Kindle

Your Slumbering Mind!

Birister Sharma

Copyright © 2022 Birister Sharma

All Rights Reserved.

Made   with   ❤on   the   Notion   Press   Platform

www.notionpress.com

Dedicated to my loving wife....

Pallabi Devi Sharma

I surrendered to you, O my Lord......

"Om Namah Shivaya"

Table of Contents

One word

Time is ticking on and on. You have no time to lay down yourself in the world of dreams. Wake up yourself before the golden opportunity will leave you forever. Nobody will wake up you. You have to wake up yourself.

Stop knitting your dreams while sleeping. Wake up and fulfil your dreams into realities. Your dreams are worthless until you will not work for your dreams.

Every passing moment is precious for you. Don't spend your priceless time only for merry-making, fun and feast. Wake up and take your own responsibility. And create your own legacy.

If you want to achieve something in your life, then utilize your time in some constructive and purposeful works.

Do something great in your life.

Wake up and move ahead…

Don't turn back until you will not reach to your final goal.

The golden opportunity is always waiting for you.

1. Be Brave

Being brave means knowing that when you fail, you don't fail forever.

---Lana Del Rey

Be brave like a lion.

A lion is a king of the forest even he is alone.

When he roars, the entire forest trembles.

What about you?

Think about yourself.

There is no place for cowards.

Only a brave man can live in this world.

Only a brave man can rule in this world.

A brave man lives every moment of his life.

But a coward dies every moment of his life.

A brave man is a symbol of immortality.

But a coward is a symbol of mortal.

Think like a brave man.

Dream like a brave man.

Imagine like a brave man.

Plan like a brave man.

Decide like a brave man.

Prepare like a brave man.

Fight like a brave man.

Talk like a brave man.

Walk like a brave man.

Work like a brave man.

A brave man never fails in his life.

Even if he fails, but he never takes his failure as ultimate;

He takes his failure as his greatest challenge.

He learns the greatest lesson from his failure, and gains more experience.

He takes revenge with his failure with his grand success.

He never quits in his life.

He fights till the last breath of his life.

He accepts to die while fighting rather than to live a mediocre life.

Be brave like a brave soldier.

A soldier when he marches for a battle, he never wants to return as a defeated soldier,

But he wants to return as a victorious soldier.

Your life is always like a big battle.

Your battle is against the tough challenges of your life.

You have to defeat them all.

You have to fight like a brave soldier.

Never surrender your life.

Once you surrender in your life, you will never witness your grand success and glory.

You are born to be brave.

But you are not born to be a coward.

---***---

2. Help Yourself

All the advice in the world will never help you until you help yourself.

---Fred Van Amburgh

Nobody can help you until you help yourself.

Only you can help yourself.

You are your own best help.

No advice ever helps you until you will not help yourself.

Your self-help is the key to your success.

Be your own helping hands.

Never depends on anybody.

Always depends on yourself.

Nobody can help you better than you yourself.

If you help yourself, it means you are acting as your best friend.

If you hold back yourself, it means you are acting as your worst foe.

A sleeping lion couldn't catch his prey;

He has to hunt for his prey.

In the similar way, if you want something in your life,

You have to help yourself.

Always remember that God helps those who help themselves.

---***---

3. Be Ambitious

*Ambition is the germ from which all growth
of nobleness proceeds.*

---Ralph Waldo Emerson

Your ambition is the key to your success and glory.

If you have no ambition, then there is no success and no glory in your life.

Your ambition is the projectile of your success and glory.

It is your guide.

It is your mentor.

A man without ambition is like a bird without wings.

Without ambition, you will reach nowhere.

Without ambition, your life is meaningless.

Without ambition, your life is directionless.

Without ambition, your life is purposeless.

It is your ambition that awakes your sleeping mind, heart and soul.

It is your ambition that unearths your hidden potentials.

Your ambition is the first step to encourage yourself.

Your ambition is the first course to uplift yourself.

Your ambition is the decision maker of your career.

You ambition plays an important role to build your bright future.

All the great men and women in this entire world are highly ambitious in their lives.

That's why they have earned great names, fames, wealth and glories in their lives.

Only an ambitious man can make the great history of his life.

Only an ambitious man can create the greatest legacy in his life.

Always be ambitious in your life in order to make your life from good to better and from better to best.

Don't live your life like an aimless creature.

Only animals live aimless lives.

If you really want to do something great in your life, then always be ambitious in your life.

---***---

4. Imagine with your entire mind

Imagination is everything. It is the preview of life's coming attractions.

---Albert Einstein

Imagine with your entire mind.

Your mind is the generator of your imagination.

Your imagination is the road map and blueprint of your success.

Your mind is a thought factory.

You can imagine anything you like.

Everything is done with the power of your imagination.

If you imagine yourself weak, you will become weak.

If you imagine yourself helpless, you will become helpless.

If you imagine yourself strong, you will become strong.

If you imagine yourself positive, you will become positive.

If you imagine yourself negative, you will become negative.

If you imagine yourself confident, you will become confident.

As you imagine yourself as you become in your life.

If you imagine success in your life, you will achieve your success.

If you imagine happiness in your life, you will realize your happiness.

If you imagine prosperity in your life, you will gain your prosperity.

If you imagine peace in your life, you will attain your peace.

Everything is possible with your imagination.

You can invent anything with the power of your imagination.

You can discover anything with the power of your imagination.

You can create anything with the power of your imagination.

You can make anything with the power of your imagination.

An architect couldn't design the model of any building if he doesn't imagine the whole structure of the building in his mind.

There is an infinite power of your imagination.

Everything happens first in your mind.

Never underestimate your imagination.

Build up the size and shape of your imagination.

---***---

5. Self-doubt is a crime

The worst enemy to creativity is self-doubt.

---Sylvia Plath

Self-doubt is a crime.

It will kill your good thoughts.

It will kill your beautiful dreams.

It will kill your great ideas.

It will kill your big plans.

It will kill your best decisions.

It will kill your best preparations.

It will kill your best actions.

Never ever doubt about yourself.

It is a big crime.

It will drain out your energy.

It will drain out your strengths.

It will drain out your powers.

It will drain out your talents.

It will drain out your skills.

It will make you weak.

It will make you helpless.

It will make you aimless.

It will make you purposeless.

It will make you hopeless.

It will ruin your beautiful life.

If you want to achieve your grand success and glory in your life, then kill your self-doubt.

Kill your self-doubt with your self-believe.

Kill your self-doubt with your self-confidence.

Kill your self-doubt with your self-esteem.

Kill your self-doubt with your self-discipline.

Kill your self-doubt with your enthusiasm.

Kill your self-doubt with your positive attitudes.

Kill your self-doubt with your perseverance.

Your self-doubt is the biggest enemy of your success and glory.

Kill it before it will kill you.

---***---

6. Laugh at your own mistakes

You grow up the first day you have your real laugh at yourself.

---Ethel Barrymore

Learn to laugh at your own mistake.

But never laugh at other's mistake.

Learn from their mistakes.

You will grow up in your life when you accept your every mistake with a broad smile.

Amend your mistake the moment you realize it.

Don't postpone it for the next day.

Your mistake is your best teacher.

Learn from it.

If you ever commit any mistake unknowingly, then it is not your fault, but it is your learning experience.

Mistake is the part of your life.

But don't commit any mistake intentionally.

It is a crime against you.

Don't repeat the same mistake again and again.

A small mistake may ruin your beautiful life.

Don't ignore any mistake in your life.

Don't leave your mistake unguarded.

An unguarded mistake is just like a naked knife; it will harm you at any moment.

Be sincere and careful in your every move and every approach.

You never know when you will commit any mistake.

A committed mistake is always a mistake, whether a small mistake or a big mistake, whether you commit your mistake by intent or not.

You never deny it.

A wise man always learns from the mistakes of other people.

But a foolish man neither learns from his mistake nor from the mistakes of other people.

How many times you commit mistake and learn from it?

Life is very short.

You have very limited time.

Before you approach to do anything in your life, observe it, research it, analyze it, and judge it critically.

Never ever try to jump blindly into anything in your life.

Take your own time.

Think about it.

Meditate on it.

Ask yourself.

Watch yourself.

Look it closely.

Then put your every step carefully and judiciously.

---***---

7. Life is a big test

Life is a big test: it tests our patience; every time brings the bite close to our mouth and then suddenly snatches it away.

---Writo Maniac

Life is a big test.

Every moment and every day is a big test for you.

You have to give the test of your life.

But don't try to run away from it.

Even if you ever succeed to flee away from it;

It will chase you wherever you go.

You will never escape from it.

If you want to witness your happiness, then life will test you with your sorrows and hardships.

If you want to witness your grand success, then life will test you with your failures and setbacks.

But don't afraid.

Give your best!

It will never make you weak and helpless, but it will make you stronger and powerful.

It will teach you how to live your life in the best possible manner.

It will guide you to face every challenge of your life.

It will give you the right direction to move ahead in your life.

It will teach you the art of living.

It will teach you the true meaning of your life.

It will teach you the true purpose of your life.

But if you ever fail to give the test of your life, then you will have to face more troubles and upheavals in your coming days, in your coming weeks, in your coming months and in your coming years.

---***---

8. Your choices

In every single thing you do, you are choosing a direction. Your life is a product of choices.

---Dr. Kathleen Hall

In your life, everything depends on your choices.

Whatever you want to become in your life, it depends on your choices.

Whatever you want in your life, it depends on your choices.

Whatever you want to do in your life, it depends on your choices.

Whoever you want to meet in your life, it depends on your choices.

If you want happiness in your life, it depends on your choices.

If you want prosperity in your life, it depends on your choices.

If you want success in your life, it depends on your choices.

If you want peace and harmony in your life, it depends on your choices.

Whatever condition you want in your life, it depends on your choices.

Whatever life you want, it depends on your choices.

Your choices are the ultimate source of your life.

You have always choices to live your life the way you want.

You never blame anyone for your choices.

You are the sole responsible for your own choices, whether good or bad, whether best or worst.

It is your own choice whether you become rich or poor.

It is your own choice whether you become wise or foolish.

It is your own choice whether you become strong or weak.

It is your own choice whether you become a winner or a loser.

It is your own choice whether you become a brave or a coward.

It is your own choice whether you become successful or unsuccessful.

It is your own choice whether you build the foundation of your house or demolish the foundation of your house.

It is your own choice what you want to discover in your life.

It is your own choice what you want to invent in your life.

It is your own choice what you want to explore in your life.

It is your own choice what you want to create in your life.

It is your own choice where you want to reach in your life.

It is your own choice what you want to achieve in your life.

It is your own choice whether you make your life beautiful or ugly.

It is your own choice whether you make your world like a heaven or like a hell.

It is your own choice whether you change yourself or not.

Everything depends on your choices.

You are the master of your own choice.

Nobody can force you to do anything without your consent.

One choice may build your life, and one choice may spoil your life.

Don't make your choice in a hurry.

Don't follow the choice of other people.

Make your own choice.

Before you make any choice in your life, take your time, think about it, ask yourself, research yourself, and judge yourself.

---***---

9. Prepare Yourself

Before anything else, preparation is the key to success.

---Alexander Graham Bell

Prepare yourself before you want to do anything in your life.

Prepare yourself before you execute anything.

Prepare yourself before you act on anything.

Prepare yourself mentally, physically and spiritually.

Your preparation is the first key to your grand success and glory.

Your preparation makes you order and discipline in your life.

Your preparation makes you aware of everything.

You will never miss your golden opportunity if you prepare yourself.

Your preparation is the first rehearsal to approach anything.

A student couldn't clear his examination without preparation.

A soldier couldn't win any battle without preparation.

An actor couldn't act brilliantly without preparation.

A musician couldn't compose any song without preparation.

A writer couldn't write his masterpiece book without preparation.

An artist couldn't paint his art without preparation.

A farmer couldn't grow his crops without preparation.

A player couldn't defeat his opponent without preparation.

A chef couldn't cook the appetizing dish without preparation.

A sailor couldn't sail his ship without preparation.

Without preparation, you couldn't achieve anything.

Without preparation, nothing is possible for you.

Your preparation is the first requisite of your life.

Prepare yourself before anything happens in your life.

It is worthless if you prepare yourself after anything happens.

Prepare your mind, heart and soul before you do anything in your life.

---***---

10. Slow and steady

Wisely and slow; - they stumble that run fast.

---William Shakespeare

Don't afraid to grow slowly and steadily in your life.

Follow the rule of slow and steady wins the race.

Don't try to run as fast as a hare.

You will stumble down in the middle of the race.

Be like a tortoise.

Slow and steady…

You will never miss anything.

You will always reach to your finishing milestone.

Believe in your pace and caliber.

Work with single minded goal.

Keep your patience.

But don't try to match your pace with the pace of other people.

Follow your own pace.

You are unique and different from them.

There is a great beauty in slow and steady.

Never get haste in your life.

Always remember that haste makes waste.

You will only enjoy your life if you are slow and steady in your every approach.

Look at around your surroundings, how the small and tiny plants and trees are growing slowly and steadily.

A small nut also grows into a huge tree in slow and steady pace.

Look at your watch, how it is ticking slowly and steadily.

The heading time never moves in a hurry, but it completes its hours in a slow and steady manner.

In the similar way, you will grow and develop slowly and steadily in your life.

You will never grow and develop overnight.

You will never achieve your success and glory in a day.

You have to wait for the right time.

You will only win the race of your life if you always work slowly and steadily.

---***---

About the author:

Birister Sharma is a full time author. He is also an avid reader. He loves reading, writing, and motivation. He has penned down dozens of self-help motivational books and novels so far.

You may contact him @ birister2007@gmail.com